INVESTMENT PROPERTY

+

TIME

=

WEALTH

Adrian Hill

SUPERIOR
ACCOUNTING GROUP
Minimise Tax | Maximise Retirement

National Library of Australia Cataloguing-in-Publication entry

Creator: Hill, Adrian Henry, 1969- author.

Title: Investment property + time = wealth / Adrian Henry Hill.

ISBN: 9780994425584 (pbk.)

Subjects: Real estate investment.
Real property.
Wealth.

Dewey Number: 332.6324

Editing, cover design and layout by OMNE Author Solutions

Printed by OMNE Publishing www.omne.com.au

Book is available in print and as an eBook.

Dedication

To my beautiful wife Anita, thanks for your input and your loving support throughout the process of writing this book and also in life. You are my best friend, one of a kind and you light up a room whenever you enter it. You are an amazing wife and an even better mother. Each day you inspire me with your energy and positivity. My life is complete with you in it. I love you always and to the moon and back.

To my gorgeous daughters Brittany and Jade, I hope that I can help and guide you both to become financially independent young women, so that you can live life to the fullest and enjoy the freedom that financial independence brings, whilst encouraging others to do the same.

About this book

"Investment Property + Time = Wealth" - fills a void in the market for a practical guide to help investors to get the most out of their investment properties.

Most people find the topics covered in this book very overwhelming, confronting and confusing. As such, the majority choose to ignore it. This is called financial neglect, which as investors we cannot do. This book is here to take away the stress and help guide the investor to ultimately achieve financial independence.

"Investment Property + Time = Wealth" is the answer to investors who have always wanted to better understand the power of investment properties, but did not know how to legally claim what they are entitled to and that property can be purchased by using your super.

As a successful investor myself, I write this book coming from a place of practical experience and credibility.

What Makes This Book Unique?

This book is written by an accountant who is passionate about investment properties. It is from his own personal investing experience and decades of dealing with the tax office, that he is able to provide fellow investors with a practical guide, full of tips and tricks, from pre-purchase through to sale. He realises that it is vitally important to minimise the holding costs of investment properties and to carefully consider what needs to be taken into account to protect all of your assets. He is on a crusade to raise awareness and have a profound impact on the amount of super that mum and dads will have in retirement - The secret ingredient is to purchase an investment property with their super.

What is the Ultimate Benefit of your Book for the Reader?

Shows you how owning investment properties, both personally and in super, can enhance your lifestyle.

It tells you how you can afford to own an investment property by maximising the tax deductions, whilst protecting and securing your assets and utilising property to significantly grow your super nest egg.

Contents

My Story

My story is a financial one but it begins in a very personal way. I met my beautiful wife Anita during the first subject of our six-and-a-half year degree at Monash University. We quickly fell in love and got married, then produced two wonderful girls who are the light of our lives.

Having a family of four at such a young age gave us some very sharp lessons in the difficulties of life. We struggled to save for our first home and, even with the help of our Nan who let us move in with her and live as cheaply as possible, it was a definite struggle. It was during this period that we learned the first of many key lessons that have helped us go from that precarious financial position to become millionaires: the only way to get ahead is to have a budget. Yes, I know many people consider the dreaded "b" word to be a dirty one but it taught us to respect money and to make sure we always know where it goes and what it is used for. In short, it put us in control of our own finances.

Our first home was a three-bedroom place in Cheltenham, 20 kilometres out of Melbourne. In hindsight, it would have been the perfect first rental property but at that stage we weren't yet able to recognise the fact. That first house was bought very much under the old school of thought, which basically states you have to work like a dog until you can afford to buy a house, and then spend the rest of your life working to pay off the mortgage.

We always felt there ought to be more to life than that but it took us a long time to find the correct path. We would spend long hours walking the dog, talking and – both being accountants – crunching the numbers but we still couldn't understand why anybody would bother to own a rental property. The rent never covers the mortgage repayments, so what's the point of owning something that continually loses money?

Then we discovered two little words that changed everything: capital growth. In fact, they're so important I'm going to write them again in big capital letters:

Capital Growth

The basic principle behind this is that the property continues to grow in value while the loan always stays the same. It gives rise to another excellent word, equity, which pretty much means getting money for nothing. I can't think of anybody who would say no to that.

Of course, harnessing this principle relies on continued capital growth and having a stable or increasing income, plus you will need to build in contingencies to ride out the short-term market fluctuations.

Obviously one of the dominant forces behind capital growth is the scarcity of land. It's a commodity that everybody in the world wants and needs, yet it's the one thing they're not making any more of and never will again. The amount of land in the world today, being shared between seven billion people, is exactly how much 10 billion people or more will have to share in fifty years' time. In fact, if the experts are right about global warming and rising sea levels there could be even less.

Therefore, it's a good bet that any property you own will increase in value. The rate of the increase constantly varies as the market moves back and forth, up and down, but there are two things you should always keep in mind:

- historically it's been shown that over a period of time property will grow at two to three per cent above inflation;
- any fall-off in prices, which does happen from time to time, can affect all property values but more so those in the middle to high-priced property markets.

You can see, then, that owning rental property gives you a double bonus: income from rent in the short term and capital growth over the long term.

Of course, our path to financial freedom was not a straight one. Because we were feeling our own way through the dark and there was nobody out there to hand us the information we needed in a neat package, like this book is giving it to you, we had a few false starts that taught us some very valuable lessons. One of those came in the early 1990s when I was working in Collingwood. We decided to move to Park Orchards and bought some land there for $125,000 that we planned to build on. After six months, though, we realised we couldn't yet afford to build our dream home so we sold it for $200,000. In that situation our inexperience cost us twice over, as the property was re-sold again six months later for $300,000 when the Eastern Freeway opened.

There are two valuable lessons to be found in that experience. The first – and I cannot possible stress this enough – is that land will always go up in value. The second, though, is that land is also very expensive to hold onto if you're not planning to build a rental property in the near future. I'll get to the reasons for that in a short while but first I want to introduce you to one of the key principles that allowed us to go from being penniless university students to millionaires. It is simply this:

Money Is A Tool

That's all. Again, it seems like a laughably simple concept, almost a trite statement really, but accepting it as a fact requires a fundamental shift in your thinking and a complete re-evaluation of your relationship to your finances. You need to see money as a means to an end, not an end in itself. Your ultimate goal is not to accumulate as much money as you can in your bank account before you die; it's to use the money that has passed through your hands in your lifetime to give you the best possible quality of life. Think of your life as a journey you are taking, a long distance car trip for instance, and money is simply the fuel that keeps you moving in much the same way as the food you consume gets you through each day. You need to be dispassionate about allocating appropriate amounts of money to your living expenses, home loan repayments, entertainment and so forth, always setting aside as much as possible for investing.

There are many different types of investing, with rental properties being the one we've dealt with most and gained the most profit from. The strategy we used worked for us because we were almost 100 per cent focused on building a business at the same time. Having read this far into the book, you would be aware of at least five other strategies to turbo-charge your wealth-creation from property.

However, there's one investment that needs to be your very first port of call on the journey to financial independence. Before you invest a cent in property, or anywhere else for that matter, you need to invest in yourself. By simply reading this book you've made an excellent start, trying as you are to benefit from the experience of those who have already made the journey you're trying to begin. Now I'll let you in on a little secret – that's exactly the same way that we started. Our practical education began back in 2000 when we started reading books just like the one you hold in your hands right now. As well as that we attended a number of seminars where we learned things they never taught us during our degrees or afterwards; we have spent close to $50,000 on self-education. It's certainly a lot of money but it's important not to dwell on that fact. The trick is to write the money off as a cost of business and think of it as an investment in yourself, which is easy for us to do as that money we initially spent has created a high enough return to make us millionaires.

It's amazing, really, to think of how much time Anita and I both spent in accounting firms without ever learning how to become financially free. You'd think it would be the first perk of a life spent juggling numbers for other people but none of our colleagues was asking the right questions and none of our superiors seemed to have the answers anyhow.

Of course, that lack of assistance turned out to be beneficial in one way, as it left us to learn everything the hard way. We passed through the school of hard knocks and picked up the skills we now have by actually doing things rather than simply observing or reading about them. For instance, nobody ever told us one of the most important equations for those undertaking a wealth-creation journey; we had to figure it out for ourselves.

It goes like this:

Asset + time = wealth

Or, to put it another way:

Property + time = wealth

Why Rental Properties?

We settled on rental properties as our wealth-creation vehicle for a number of reasons including:

- the benefits of capital growth and equity;

- good debt versus bad debt (we wanted assets that appreciate and/or earn income, not those that depreciate and/or lose income);

- the tendency for rents to double every decade;

- the fact that 30 per cent of Australians currently rent with more likely to do so in the future;

- a high income is generally not needed to buy an income property; and

- value can be added easily by renovating.

But by far the best reason of all is that the tenant and the tax man – that's right, the tax man – help you pay for the rental property. Let's look at how.

How To Get Help Owning Your Rental Property

If you keep the property in excellent condition you will get the maximum amount of rent from your tenant, which can be put towards paying down your mortgage. The tax man's part, though, is a little more complicated and can be a lot more profitable to your bottom line.

There are two things I should mention before proceeding: you should avoid buying vacant land, unless you intend to immediately build a rental property on it, develop it or add value in some other way, because unless your property is producing an income you won't get the many excellent tax benefits I'm going to spell out for you. Also, you should keep in mind that owning two smaller rental properties is better than owning one big one.

If you have a solid understanding of tax law or, even better, have a good accountant who knows it backwards, you can claim many tax deductions that will significantly increase your wealth and hasten your journey towards financial freedom. The key words there, of course, are "good accountant". You might think it's reasonable to assume that all accountants would know what I'm about to tell you but unfortunately that is not the case. The education received by accountants, both at university and throughout their on-site training, is patchy at best so you have to be extremely careful about choosing one that can not only talk the talk but also walk the walk.

It was this realisation that actually led us to create our business, Superior Accounting Solutions Pty Ltd, because we recognised a massive gap in the market that simply wasn't being filled by the majority of accountants who were out there.

It's not just an accountant that you need as you begin your journey to financial freedom, either. You need to build an entire team to support you along the way and help you reach your goals, each member of which will play a crucial role. Team members should include:

- accountant
- mortgage broker / financier
- property manager
- insurance broker
- solicitor
- quantity surveyor

Section 1:

Tax Minimisation

Chapter 1:
Tax Deductions Generally
& Your Share of Rental Income and Expenses

As accountants, there are lots of tricks we can share with you to help buy-and-hold your property, particularly in regard to maximising your tax deductions and asset protection. To start at the very beginning, an item is tax deductible if it is an expense incurred (that is, paid) while you were earning income.

If you're not sure if an expense is tax deductible simply keep the tax invoice and seek your accountant's advice when your tax return is being prepared. The accountant should be on your side and will try to claim as much as possible to allow you to minimise your tax each year. It's their job to be proactive in this area and it's your right to claim everything you're entitled to.

RENTAL PROPERTY TAX ISSUES IN GENERAL

Rental income is, as you would expect, the income you receive in rent from your tenant each financial year.

HINT FOR TAX RETURN

If you do not receive your rent for June 2015 until 1 July, that rent is not income in the 2015 tax year but will be included in the 2016 tax year

Your share of rental income and expenses

Your share of rental income and expenses is divided up according to who legally owns the property. For instance, property can be owned as:

- joint tenants, who each hold an equal interest in the property;

- tenants in common, who may hold unequal interests in the property. One could have an 80 per cent interest and the other 20 per cent.

HINT FOR TAX RETURN

Your rental income and expenses must be allocated to each according to their legal interest in the property, no matter what agreements they make between themselves.

Rental expenses

You can claim a deduction for certain expenses you pay during the period your property is being rented or is available for rent.

There are three types of rental expenses:

1. Expenses that cannot be claimed as deductions;

2. Immediate deductions, which can be claimed in the financial year that you pay them;

3. Deductions expensed over a number of financial years.

Chapter 2:
Deductions not Immediately Claimable:
Purchase Costs & Sale Costs

Purchase and sale costs

You cannot claim a deduction for the costs of purchasing or selling your rental property. However, they may form part of the cost base of the property for Capital Gains Tax (CGT) purposes. Below is an example that shows the kind of expenses you can claim as part of the cost base:

Purchase details:

Date of signing contract: 19 July

Date of settlement: 19 September

Purchase price	$300,000
Stamp Duty	$15,000
Legal costs	$1,000
Travel to purchase property	$2,000
Building inspection	$500
Pest inspection	$500
Buyer's agent fees	$6,000
Total Purchase Costs	**$325,000**

This means that when the above property is sold, $325,000 will be included in the cost base from which the amount of any capital gain or capital loss will be figured out.

HINT FOR TAX RETURN

The signing date of the contract is the triggering point for Capital Gains Tax purposes, while the settlement date is the triggering point for depreciation to start. Your total purchase costs, when you sell the property, may be reduced by depreciation and building write-off claimed.

Chapter 3:
Immediate Deductions:
Body Corporate Fees & Interest Paid on Loans

Immediate deductions are those that can be claimed in the same financial year as they have been paid. Examples include:

- advertising for tenants
- bank fees
- body corporate fees and charges *
- cleaning
- council rates
- electricity and gas
- gardening and lawn mowing
- gifts to tenants and/or property managers
- in-house audio/video service charges
- insurance (including building, contents and public liability)
- interest on loans *
- Land Tax
- lease document expenses (including preparation, registration and stamp duty)
- legal expenses * (excluding acquisition costs and borrowing costs)
- mortgage discharge expenses *
- pest (annual check)

- property agent's fees and commission
- quantity surveyor's fees
- repairs and maintenance *
- security patrol fees
- servicing costs – for example, servicing a water heater
- stationery and postage
- telephone calls and line rental
- travel and car expenses for rent collection, property inspection and maintenance*
- water rates and charges.

Items marked with an asterisk (*) are discussed in detail overleaf.

HINT FOR TAX RETURN

You can only claim these expenses if you pay for them and are not reimbursed by the tenant

Body corporate fees and charges

Body corporate fees apply when you own an apartment, unit or any dwelling that has common property. The body corporate is responsible for the upkeep of the common property – such as lawns, driveways and lifts – as well as sometimes for the maintenance of external walls. It will usually issue a quarterly invoice to cover the costs of the above. These contributions are, in the majority of cases, covering a "general purpose sinking fund" and are fully claimable when paid.

A general purpose sinking fund is one that's established to cover a variety of unspecified expenses (some of which may be capital expenses) that are paid by the body corporate in maintaining the common property. This generally involves things like painting the common property and repairing or replacing fixtures and fittings. These are immediately deductible.

What is not immediately deductible, however, is if the body corporate requires you to make payments to a "special purpose fund" to pay for particular capital expenditure. A special purpose fund is set up to cover a specified, generally significant, expense that is not covered by ongoing contributions to a general purpose sinking fund. Most special purpose funds are established to cover the cost of capital improvement to the common property.

HINT FOR TAX RETURN

These special purpose contributions generally will be claimable at the rate of 2.50 per cent per annum.

Interest on loans

If you take out a loan to purchase a rental property, you can claim the interest charged on that loan as a deduction. The important thing to be aware of here is that the deductibility of the interest depends entirely on what the money was used for. Incidentally, what property is secured against the loan is irrelevant when figuring out the deductibility of the interest.

While the property is being rented, or is available for rent, you may also claim interest charged on loans taken out for the following purposes:

- to purchase depreciating assets
- for repairs
- for renovations.

HINT FOR TAX RETURN

You have to keep your personal loans entirely separate from the loans you intend to be tax deductible. To give an example, if you buy a property for a total cost of $325,000 (which included a contract price of $300,000) the bank would normally give you an 80 per cent loan, secured against that property, of $240,000. You need to finance the remaining $85,000 from elsewhere. If you take out a loan for that amount, then make sure that no money for personal purposes is ever withdrawn or deposited into it; you can claim the interest on both loans against any rent received from the property.

Similarly, if you take out a loan to purchase land on which to build a rental property or to finance renovations to a property you intend to rent out, the interest on the loan will be deductible from the time you take the loan out. However, if your intention changes – if, for example, you decide to move into the property yourself or you no longer intend to use it to produce rent or other income – you cannot claim the interest after your intention changes

HINT FOR TAX RETURN

Interest is not the only expense you can claim in the period between buying the land and building a rental property on it. You can also claim other holding costs such as water rates, land tax, lawn mowing, council rates and insurance

Where personal and property loans are combined

The first thing I have to say about combining personal and property loans is that you shouldn't do it. Your accounting will be much simpler if you are able to keep the two entirely separate. For instance, if you take out a loan to buy a rental property and a private car you have to divide the interest on the loan into deductible and non-deductible parts depending on how much each item cost.

If you have a loan account that has a fluctuating balance due to a variety of deposits and withdrawals, and it is used for both private and rental property purposes, you must keep accurate records so you can calculate the interest that applies to the rental property portion of the loan. In other words, you need to figure out how much interest you paid as part of earning income through rent (which is deductible) and how much you paid as part of the personal loan (which is not).

HINT FOR TAX RETURN

You can see now why I always suggest keeping your deductible debt totally separate from your non-deductible debt. It is time consuming and costly for you or your accountant to determine the correct amount of interest claimable. It's an area where the tax office often finds errors and therefore it is crucial to get it right.

Example: Apportionment of interest

You decide to use your bank account to take out a loan of $355,000 from which $325,000 is used to buy a rental property and $30,000 is used to buy a private car. To determine the claim using a loan interest rate of 6.75% per annum, and assuming that the property is rented from 1 July:

Interest for year one = $355,000   X   6.75% = $23,963

Apportionment of interest payment related to rental property:

Total interest expense	X	rental property loan / total borrowings	=	Deductible interest
$23,963	X	$325,000 / $355,000	=	$21,938

Where you purchase a new home to live in and keep your old one to rent out

Some rental property owners borrow money to buy a new home and then rent out their previous home. If there is an outstanding loan on the old home and that property is used to produce income, the interest outstanding on the loan – or at least part of it – will be deductible.

However, an interest deduction cannot be claimed on the loan used to buy the new home because it is not used to produce income. This is the case regardless of whether the loan for the new home is secured against the former home.

Example – Old house rented

You bought your home five years ago for $275,000 (including all costs). The loan was $250,000 at the time of purchase but is now down to $100,000. The house is now worth $500,000.

You buy a new home for $450,000 (including all costs), using two loans to complete the purchase. One is for $360,000, secured against the new home, and the other is for $90,000, secured against the old home. You move into the new property and rent out your old home.

The only interest claimable is that from the $100,000 loan, which is being used for the purpose of creating income.

HINT FOR TAX RETURN

If I was purchasing a home in the future I would always utilise an offset account loan type, which is explained in greater detail a little further.

The Main Types of Loan Products Utilised by Rental Property Investors

Line of Credit (LOC)/Redraws

A line of credit is a loan, similar to a credit card, which can be drawn up to a pre-determined maximum limit. Interest is only charged on the drawn balance and not on the available (undrawn) balance. For the interest to be deductible, you have to make sure there is a clear distinction between the business and personal uses of the loan.

For example, you might set up a $100,000 LOC, secured against your private home. If you use this to help you buy a rental property, the interest will be deductible against the rent received from your property. Your aunt passes away, leaving you $20,000 that you deposit into the LOC, dropping the balance to $80,000. You then dip back into the loan, taking $20,000 out to buy a boat for your personal use and bringing the balance back up to $100,000.

By doing this you've effectively created two loans, one of $80,000 that is tax deductible against the income received from your property and one of $20,000 that is not. You've turned $20,000 of deductible debt into non-deductible debt, which isn't good and demonstrates how careful you need to be when moving money around.

Making it even more difficult is the fact the tax office won't let you allocate repayments solely against the boat loan. If you choose to pay $1,000 into the above LOC it would be deemed to be reducing the boat loan by $200 ($1,000 x 20 per cent) and the rental property loan by $800 ($1,000 x 80 per cent).

Line of Credit (LOC) versus offset account

There is another way you could have proceeded with the previous example, one that would have been far more advantageous.

When you receive the $20,000 from your aunt's estate, instead of depositing it into the $100,000 LOC you could put it into a separate account held by the same bank. The bank can then "offset" the interest charged to you on the $100,000 loan against the interest they would pay you on the $20,000 deposit being held in the offset account.

Instead of paying the interest on $100,000 and receiving interest on $20,000, you will only have to pay the interest on $80,000. To put it another way, the $20,000 in your offset account gets subtracted from the $100,000 in your LOC before any interest in calculated.

You can then buy the $20,000 boat from the offset account, leaving the original $100,000 loan fully intact.

I favour offset accounts because they keep your interest deduction options as open as possible, particularly when you're going to pay a loan down by depositing money into it.

You should even set up an offset account on your private home loan, so you can maximise the interest deductions if you ever decide to rent it out in the future. Even if you don't think you will ever rent it out, you're keeping your options open and that's always a good thing.

Chapter 4:
Immediate Deductions:
Legal Expenses & Repairs and Maintenance

Legal expenses

Some legal expenses incurred in producing your rental income are deductible, such as the cost of evicting a non-paying tenant.

Most legal expenses, however, are of a capital nature and are therefore not deductible. These include the costs of purchasing or selling your property and defending your title to the property. It's not all bad news, though. Non-deductible legal expenses may form part of the cost base of your property for Capital Gains Tax purposes.

Example: Deductible legal expenses

In August 2014 your tenants moved out owing four weeks' rent. You retained the bond money and took the tenants to court to terminate the lease and recover the balance of the rent. The legal expenses are fully deductible because they were incurred while seeking to recover assessable rental income and you wished to continue earning income from the property.

HINT FOR TAX RETURN

You must include the retained bond money and the recovered rent as assessable income in the financial year received.

Mortgage discharge expenses

These are the costs involved in discharging a mortgage other than through payments of principal and interest. Mortgage discharge expenses may include penalty interest payments, early termination fees or deferred establishment fees. They're claimable in the year they are paid.

Repairs and maintenance

Repairs can generally be categorised into two types:

1. Repairs that are immediately claimable

2. Repairs that are depreciable.

Immediately claimable repairs

These repairs must directly relate to wear and tear or other damage that occurred as a result of you renting out the property.

They generally involve the replacement or renewal of a worn-out or broken part, such as guttering torn down during a storm or part of a fence that was damaged by a falling tree branch.

A repair simply restores the item to its original state prior to it needing to be fixed.

Some of the repairs you can claim deductions for include replacing broken windows, maintaining plumbing and repairing electrical appliances.

HINT FOR TAX RETURN

You need to consider how long you have been renting out the property before a repair is deemed to be from the wear and tear associated with the use of the tenant

Depreciable repairs

The following expenses are depreciable at the rate of 2.50 per cent per annum:

- the replacement of an entire structure or unit of property, such as a complete fence or set of kitchen cupboards;

- improvements, renovations, extensions and alterations;

- initial repairs, which means fixing defects and repairing damage that existed in the property on the date you acquired it.

Example: Improvements

You've been renting a property out for a number of years when a section of the timber fence – not the entire fence but only part of it – comes apart and needs replacing. If you replace the timber fence with a Colorbond fence it is deemed to be an improvement rather than a repair.

Example: Initial repairs

You need to make some repairs to your newly acquired rental property before the first tenants move in. You pay an interior decorator to repaint dirty walls, replace broken light fittings and repair doors on two bedrooms. You also discover white ants in some of the floorboards, which requires white ant treatment and replacement of some of the boards.

It is considered that these expenses were incurred to make the property suitable for rental and did not arise from your use of the property to generate rental income.

General guide to claiming repairs

Repairs to a rental property will generally be claimable if:

- the property continues to be rented on an ongoing basis; or

- the property remains available for rent but there is a short period when the property is unoccupied, such as when unseasonable weather causes cancellations of bookings or advertising is unsuccessful in attracting tenants.

If you no longer rent the property, the cost of repairs may still be deductible provided:

- the need for the repairs is related to the period in which the property was used by you to produce income; and

- the property was producing income during the financial year in which you paid for the repairs.

Example: Repairs when the property is no longer rented out

August 2014 – Your tenants move out.

September 2014 – You discover the stove doesn't work, kitchen tiles are cracked and the toilet window is broken. You also discover a hole in a bedroom wall that had been covered with a poster.

October 2014 – You pay for this damage to be repaired.

Despite the fact that the property is no longer being rented out, you can still claim the repairs to the property. This is because the repairs relate to the period when the property was being rented and the repairs were completed before the end of the financial year in which the property ceased to be rented out.

HINT FOR TAX RETURN

You need to have some rental income in the same financial year that you claim the repairs. This applies even if you use the property as your home after the tenants move out.

Chapter 5:
Immediate Deductions:
Travel Expenses & Prepaid Expenses

Travel expenses

You can travel to inspect, maintain your property or collect the rent and you may be able to claim the costs of doing so.

Potential claimable travel expenses:

- airfares (retain boarding pass and ticket)
- taxi, bus and train fares
- accommodation
- phone calls
- meals
- parking costs and bridge tolls
- car hire and petrol
- cents per kilometre usage of your own car.

Example: Cents per kilometre usage of your own car

Although your local rental property is managed by a property agent, you decide to inspect the property three months after the tenants move in. During the income year you also make a number of visits to the property to carry out minor repairs. You travel 162 kilometres during the course of these visits.

At the rate of 76 cents per kilometre for your 2.6 litre car, you can claim the following deduction:

Distance x rate per km = deductible travelled amount

162 kms x 76 cents per km = $123.12

On your way to cricket each Saturday, you also drive past the property to "keep an eye on things". These trips are not deductible in any way because inspecting the property is incidental to the primary purpose of enjoying the cricket.

Apportionment of travel expenses

You are allowed a full claim where the sole purpose of the trip relates to the rental property. However, in other circumstances you may not be able to claim a deduction or you may be entitled to only a partial deduction.

If you fly to inspect your rental property, stay overnight and return home on the following day, all of the airfare and accommodation expenses can be claimed as long as the sole purpose of your trip is to inspect the property.

Where travel related to your rental property is combined with a holiday or other private activities, you may need to apportion the expenses.

If this is the case you need to take into account the reasons for your trip. If the main purpose of your trip is to have a holiday and the inspection of the property is incidental to that main purpose, you cannot claim a deduction for the cost of the travel. However, you may be able to claim local expenses directly related to the property inspection and a proportion of accommodation expenses.

Example: Apportionment of travel expenses

You own a rental property in Cairns on the north coast of Queensland. You spend $1,000 on airfares and $1,500 on accommodation when you travel from your home in Melbourne, mainly for the purpose of holidaying but also to inspect the property. You also spend $50 on taxi fares for the return trip from the hotel to the rental property. One day of your 10-day holiday (10 per cent) is spent on matters relating to the rental property and nine days (90 per cent) swimming and sightseeing.

No deduction can be claimed for any part of the $1,000 airfares but $50 can be claimed for the taxi fare.

Given that 10 per cent of the holiday is spent attending to the rental property, a deduction for 10 per cent of the accommodation expenses ($150 in this case) would be considered reasonable. The total in travel expenses you can claim is therefore $200 ($50 taxi fare plus $150 accommodation).

Prepaid expenses

If you prepay a rental property expense – such as interest – that covers a period of 12 months or less and the period ends on or before 30 June, you can claim an immediate deduction.

Example: Prepaid expenses

In June 2015 you pay interest in advance of $16,000 on a loan for your rental property, which represents the interest you would pay in an entire year. Because you pay it in June 2015, and because it relates to a period of no more than 12 months, you can claim the interest in the 2015 financial year.

HINT FOR TAX RETURN

The interest has to actually be paid to the bank before 30 June to be claimed in that year. That means you will need to allow an appropriate amount of time for you to contact your lender, have your lender agree to this, send out the paperwork for the pre-payment and for the payment to be made.

Pre-payments can be made and claimed for rental properties owned by:

1. An individual

2. Individuals jointly or as tenants in common.

Pre-payments cannot be made and claimed for rental properties owned by:

1. Trusts

2. Companies

3. Super funds.

Chapter 6:
Deductions over Several Years:
Borrowing Expenses

If the total deductible borrowing expenses are $100 or less, they are fully deductible in the income year they are incurred. However, if your total borrowing expenses are more than $100, the deduction is either spread over five years or the term of the loan – whichever is less.

These are some of the expenses directly incurred in taking out a loan for the property:

- loan establishment fees

- title search fees

- mortgage broker fees

- Stamp Duty charged on the mortgage

- valuation fees

- mortgage insurance.

HINT FOR TAX RETURN

If you repay the loan early and in less than five years, you can claim a deduction for the balance of the borrowing expenses in the year of repayment.

If you obtained the loan part way through the income year, the deduction for the first year will be apportioned according to the number of days in the year that you had the loan.

Example: Borrowing expenses

To buy a rental property for $300,000 you secure a 25-year loan of $316,000. You pay a total of $3,670 in various expenses, including establishment fees and Stamp Duty. Because these expenses are greater than $100 they must be spread out over five years or until the end of the loan, according to whichever comes first.

If you obtain the loan on 17 July 2014, you would work out the borrowing expense deduction for the first year as follows:

PRE-PAID BORROWING EXPENSES			
Mortgage Stamp Duty	$1,264		
Registration fee	$70		
Establishment fee	$700		
Settlement fee	$200		
Mortgage insurance	$1,436		
	$3,670		
	Days in year	**Claim**	**Balance**
30 June 2015	350	$703	$2,967
30 June 2016	366	$735	$2,232
30 June 2017	365	$733	$1,499
30 June 2018	365	$733	$766
30 June 2019	365	$733	$33
30 June 2020	16	$ 33	–
	1,827	**$3,670**	

HINT FOR TAX RETURN

If you refinance the above property on 30 June 2016, the remaining borrowing costs yet to be claimed – in this case $2,232 – can be written off in full when the refinance happens.

A new calculation (similar to the one above over five years) will also need to be done for the new loan that is going to pay out the old loan.

Chapter 7:
Deductions over Several Years:
Depreciation

Deduction for depreciating assets

This is one of the most attractive benefits from a tax deduction point of view, particularly as it's one of those that is often overlooked even by professionals.

Depreciation is a tax deduction that you get each year, without having to spend a cent. It's built into the purchase price of the property.

Depreciation is meant to reflect the fact that the assets are worth less as time goes by, simply because of the "wear and tear" associated with having tenants use them.

Even if a property is 15-20 years old when you buy it there can still be some fantastic depreciation benefits available to you as the purchaser. It depends on how much you pay for the property and what plant and equipment are in it at the time of purchase.

Items of interest would include:

- stove

- oven

- hot plates

- hot water service

- curtains

- light fittings

- blinds

- ducted heating

- dishwasher

- ducted cooling

- stand alone heating unit

- stand alone air-conditioning unit

- security system

- carpet

A quantity surveyor is the best option to determine your depreciation entitlements. The difference between a good quantity surveyor and an average one can have a substantial impact on the depreciation and building write-off that is claimable. This applies to both the level of detail provided in the report as well as the dollar value you can get out of a genuine professional.

Trust me; you will want to get a decent quantity surveyor. Valuers, real estate agents, accountants and solicitors generally won't have the skills and experience to get you everything you're entitled to.

A quantity surveyor's fees are also tax deductible in the year they are paid for.

Personal experience

I can speak from my own personal experience and say that quantity surveyors truly are a gift from the tax office.

We had recently bought our first rental property and were sitting outside one sunny afternoon reading *Australian Property Investor* magazine when we came across an article about quantity surveyors. We were stunned. Could the tax office really be that generous? We were both accountants; why had we never heard of this?

We researched the topic and, sure enough, discovered one of the most wonderful little tools available. At the time we were both working for a family company that owned 40 service stations throughout Victoria, so we kept researching and discovered that it applied to commercial property as well as residential. Some time later we were able to give our employers an extra one million dollars in their pockets after tax.

It made us realise there aren't many accountants out there who know everything that will help you with your rental properties. That's when Superior Accounting Solutions Pty Ltd was created.

HINT FOR TAX RETURN

The tax deductions available through depreciation and building write-off can significantly reduce the holding costs of the property. This is one reason why Superior Accounting Solutions Pty Ltd amends, on average, 80 per cent of our new clients' tax returns.

Amended tax returns are now restricted in the majority of cases to two years, which is why it's imperative that your accountant is looking after your interests.

Example: The difference a good quantity surveyor can make

One of my clients commissioned an average quantity surveyor who was relatively cheap. They got the following results:

- property purchased for $150,000 in January 1997
- has three bedrooms and a study, as well as ducted heating, dishwasher, carpet, curtains, stove, oven, range hood, etc.
- built in 1987 and still had all original fixtures and fittings
- total depreciation calculated by quantity surveyor: **$13,639**
- total building write-off calculated by quantity surveyor: **$45,354** ($1,814 per annum).

I, on the other hand, spent a little extra money and commissioned a good quantity surveyor to achieve the following results:

- property purchased for $210,000 in June 2001
- built in 1987 and still had all original fixtures and fittings

- has three bedrooms and a study, as well as ducted heating, dishwasher, security system, carpet, curtains, stove, oven, range hood, etc.

- total depreciation calculated by quantity surveyor: **$53,615**

- total building write-off calculated by quantity surveyor: **$12,873** ($1,126 per annum).

Given that approximately 60 per cent of depreciation is claimed back in the first five years, the above example means the following:

Average quantity surveyor – Claims over five years:

$13,639 x 60 per cent	=	$8,183
$1,814 x 5	=	$9,070
Total Claims		**$17,253**

Good quantity surveyor – Claims over five years:

$53,615 x 60 per cent	=	$32,169
$1,126 x 5	=	$5,630
Total Claims		**$37,799**
Difference in claims over five years	=	**$20,546**
Tax savings foregone at 31.50 per cent	=	**$6,472**

(Cashflow lost by average surveyor)

This clearly highlights the importance of a good quantity surveyor but, even more than that, it shows the cost of not using a quantity surveyor at all.

How do you work out your depreciation deduction?

There are two methods of calculating depreciation:

1. **Diminishing value method**
2. **Prime cost method.**

The **diminishing value method** assumes that the decline in value each year is a constant proportion of the remaining value, thereby producing a progressively smaller decline over time.

For depreciating assets bought after 10 May 2006, you generally use the following formula to work out the decline using the diminishing value method:

$$\text{base value (asset's cost)} \quad X \quad \frac{\text{days held}}{365} \quad X \quad \frac{200\%}{\text{asset's effective life}}$$

Example:

You buy a dishwasher for $1,000 on 1 August 2014. Assuming its operational life expectancy is 10 years, it has a depreciation rate of 20 per cent under the diminishing value method.

Year 1

$1,000 x 334/365 x 20% = $183 ($1,000 – $183 = $817)

Year 2

$817   x 365/365 x 20% = $163 ($817 - $163 = $654)

Year 3

$654   x 365/365 x 20% = $131 ($654 - $131 = $523)

The **prime cost method**, on the other hand, assumes the value of a depreciating asset decreases uniformly over its effective life. The formula for working out decline in value using the prime cost method is:

$$\text{asset's cost} \quad X \quad \frac{\text{days held}}{365} \quad X \quad \frac{100\%}{\text{asset's effective life}}$$

Example:

You buy a dishwasher for $1,000 on 1 August 2014. Assuming its operational life expectancy is 10 years, it has a depreciation rate of 10 per cent under the prime cost method.

Year 1

$1,000 x 334/365 x 10% = $92 ($1,000 – $92 = $908)

Year 2

$1,000 x 365/365 x 10% = $100 ($908 - $100 = $808)

Year 3

$1,000 x 365/365 x 10% = $100 ($808 - $100 = $708)

HINT FOR TAX RETURN

Due to the fact that rental properties usually cost more to hold in the first few years, we recommend using the diminishing value method as this will maximise your depreciation claim each year and increase your tax refund

Effective life

Generally, the effective life of a depreciating asset is how long it can be used for a taxable purpose.

Immediate deduction for certain non-business depreciating assets costing $300 or less

You can get an immediate deduction for the cost of an asset if its purchase price was under $300. This deduction is available if the asset meets all the following tests:

- it cost $300 or less

- you use it mainly for the purpose of obtaining rental income

- it is not one of a number of identical, or substantially identical, assets that together cost more than $300 (example below).

Example: Immediate deduction

You buy a blind for your rental property at a cost of $70. You can claim an immediate deduction as the blind is used to obtain rental income.

Example: No immediate deduction

You buy four blinds costing $90 each for your rental property. You cannot claim an immediate deduction for any of these because they are identical, or substantially identical, and the combined cost is more than $300.

HINT FOR TAX RETURN

In the previous example, you should have bought three of the blinds in one year and one in the next year. Then you could have fully claimed them in the respective financial years they were bought and paid for

Low-value pooling

A low-value pool is a simplified method of depreciating any assets that cost less than $1,000 per item. These assets are allocated to the pool each year and stay there once they've been added. The pool shows one cumulative dollar value for all the assets inside it, along with one depreciation amount for the entire pool.

This compares to the traditional method of showing a depreciation schedule with individual assets listed separately, each with its own depreciation calculation per year.

For the income year you initially purchase an asset, you work out its depreciation at a rate of 18.75 per cent. For the following years the deduction uses a diminishing value rate of 37.5 per cent.

Example: Depreciation claim – low-value pool

On 1 August 2014 you bought a blind for $400 and two air-conditioners for $900 each on 30 June 2015.

2015 financial year depreciation claim:

$400	x	18.75%	=	$75
$900	x	18.75%	=	$169
$900	x	18.75%	=	$169
Total Depreciation Claimed			**=**	**$413**

Low-value pool totals are:

Total items bought during year	$2,200
Less: Depreciation claim per above	($413)
Closing Value Of Pool	**$1,787**

2016 financial year depreciation claim:

Opening Value Of Pool	=	$1,787
$1,787 x 37.50%	=	$670
Total Depreciation Claimed	**=**	**$670**

Low-value pool totals are:

Opening Value Of Pool	$1,787
Total Items Bought During Year	$0
Less: Depreciation Claim Per Above	($670)
Closing Value Of Pool	**$1,117**

HINT FOR TAX RETURN

It does not matter if an asset costing under $1,000 is bought at the start or end of the financial year because the depreciation claim will be the same. A good accountant will be vigilant in moving applicable depreciation items to the low-value pool to maximise your depreciation claims each year.

Capital Works Deductions (Building Write-Off)

You can claim building (construction) expenditure over 25 or 40 years.

Examples of building expenditure include:

- plumbing
- electrical
- roofing
- slab
- carpentry
- bricklaying
- architect's and engineer's fees
- frame
- a building or an extension, such as adding a room, garage, patio or pergola
- alterations, such as removing or adding an internal wall
- structural improvements to the property, such as adding a gazebo, carport, sealed driveway, retaining wall or fence.

Examples of building expenditure not included:

- the cost of the land on which the rental property is built

- expenditure on clearing the land prior to construction

- expenditure on landscaping.

HINT FOR TAX RETURN

No claim is available until the construction is complete and you can only claim deductions for the period during the year(s) that the property is rented or is available for rent.

The claim percentage available is determined by figuring out when construction was first started. That means, from the date the foundations were laid.

Summary of building write-off claim percentage

Date construction started	Percentage rate of claim each year
17 July 1985 – 15 September 1987	4 per cent
After 15 September 1987	2.50 per cent

Estimating construction costs

Where a new owner is unable to precisely determine the construction costs of a building, an estimate from an appropriately qualified person may be used. As discussed earlier, this person would ideally be a quantity surveyor.

Chapter 8:
Worksheet Example of All Claimable Rental Deductions

You are now in a position to put together all the information you need for your tax return, as well as to determine how much you have made from your rental property in a year and how much you've paid to hold onto it.

Income	$
Rental income	14,500
Bond money refunded in lieu of rent	800
Gross rent	**15,300**
Expenses	
Advertising for tenants	98
Bank charges	100
Body corporate fees and charges	600
Borrowing expenses **	359
Cleaning	200
Council rates	800
Depreciation claim **	3,896
Gardening/lawn mowing	450
Gifts to tenant/agent	400
Gas and electricity	200
Insurance	695
Interest on loan(s)	12,475
Land Tax	300

Legal expenses	250
Pest control	150
Property agent fees/commission	1,200
Quantity surveyor's fees	660
Repairs and maintenance	1,500
Building write-off claim **	3,745
Stationery, telephone and postage	80
Travel expenses	536
Water charges	250
Sundry expenses	195
Total expenses	**29,139**
Net rental loss ($29,139 – $15,300)	**13,839**

** These items should be worked out each year by your accountant

Chapter 9:
Capital Gains Tax (CGT)
When You Sell Your Property
& Keeping Records

Our strategy has always been to buy-and-hold rental properties. However, no rule is without its exceptions and on two occasions it was the right decision to sell properties.

As a result we needed to work out how much money we would make on the sale (known as a capital gain) or what loss, if any, was incurred (known as a capital loss). This applied to us because we had purchased our property after 19 September 1985. If you bought your house before this date you would be exempt from Capital Gains Tax in the majority of cases.

Capital gain basically means that you receive more money from the sale of your rental property than the total you paid for it. A capital loss, on the other hand, means that the base cost of the property exceeds the amount you ultimately receive for it.

If you are a co-owner of an investment property, your capital gain or loss will be figured out in accordance with the percentage of your ownership interest in the property.

See overleaf for a detailed example.

Here is our most recent capital gain calculation as an example:

Purchase details:

Date of signing contract: 19 July 2005
Date of settlement: 19 September 2005

Purchase price	$300,000
Stamp Duty	$15,000
Legal costs	$1,000
Travel to purchase property	$2,000
Building inspection	$500
Pest inspection	$500
Buyer's agent fees	$6,000
Total Purchase Costs	**$325,000**

Sale details:

Date of signing contract: 19 June 2015
Date of settlement: 19 August 2015

Sales price	$500,000
Sales commission	$(15,000)
Advertising	$(3,000)
Legal costs	$(1,000)

Total Net Sales Proceeds	**$481,000**

Net capital gain is:

Net sales proceeds		$481,000
Less: Total purchase price	$325,000	
Less: depreciation and building write-off claimed *	$(23,000)	$302,000
Net capital gain		**$179,000**

As we owned the property jointly between ourselves, the net capital gain was reduced by a 50 per cent discount from $179,000 to $89,500. We each declared Capital Gain Income of $44,750 in our respective personal tax returns.

* Building write-off and depreciation claimed during the ownership period is $23,000

HINT FOR TAX RETURN ONE

Depending on who owns the property – if, for instance, it's owned by an individual(s) or a trust – the net capital gain can be reduced by a 50 per cent discount. To get the discount the property needs to be owned for more than one year from purchase contract date to sales contract date.

If a company owns the property it is not entitled to the 50 per cent discount.

HINT FOR TAX RETURN TWO

Most accountants don't believe in the benefit of claiming the depreciation and building write-off, as they are both added back at the time of sale as shown above.

However, we believe that as long as the property is held, from purchase contract to sales contract, for at least one year, you will always be in front by *claiming your entitlement.*

To demonstrate using facts from the previous example:

Depreciation and building write-off claimed for the period of ownership	$23,000
Depreciation and building write-off added back at sale	$23,000
Less: 50 per cent discount available at sale	($11,500)
Actual amount added back at sale	**$11,500**

Therefore, you are $11,500 better off by claiming your depreciation and building write-off.

HOW TO DEFER YOUR CAPITAL GAINS TAX

Using the previous example, because the sales contract was signed in June 2015 the capital gain needs to be declared as income in the 2015 tax year. This is despite the fact that the sale did not settle until August 2015.

It would have been better to move (defer) the capital gain into the next tax year. As the capital gain is taken from the date both parties sign the contract and not settlement, it would be great to lock the purchaser in to the deal but defer the gain until next year.

You need to contact a solicitor who understands this type of transaction. You enter a simultaneous put and call option contract that works as follows:

- you give the buyer a put option to sell your property to the purchaser, which is not exercisable before 1 July and expires by the end of August;

- the buyer takes a call option to be able to purchase the property from you after 1 July but they must exercise the option by the end of August;

- the normal sale of property contract is attached to the option agreements;

- you now have the right to sell your property after 1 July and the purchaser has the option to buy the property after 1 July;

- when either party exercises their option after 1 July, the contracts are officially signed and dated by each party;

- therefore, the contract date now falls after 1 July and into the next tax year.

Keeping records - Capital gains tax

You must keep records relating to your ownership of the property, including all the costs of acquiring and disposing of it, for five years after the date it is sold.

You must keep records that include:

- the date you acquired the asset
- the date you disposed of the asset
- the date you received anything in exchange for the asset
- the parties involved
- any amount that would form part of the cost base of the asset
- whether you have claimed an income tax deduction for an item of expenditure.

Keeping records - Generally

You should always keep records of both income and expenses relating to your rental property, for at least five years after you lodge your tax return.

Records of rental expenses must include:

- name of the supplier
- amount of the expense
- nature of the goods or services
- date the expense was incurred
- date of the document.

If a document does not show the payment date you can use independent evidence, such as a bank statement, to show the date the expense was incurred.

Chapter 10:
Issues for the Future & Overcoming Fears

Rental property ownership is a long-term strategy. Buying and holding is the common strategy for passive investors like the majority of us. Given that it costs around five to six per cent of the purchase price to buy and around three to four per cent of the sales price to sell, property needs to be held long-term to allow these costs to be absorbed by the property's growth in value.

Sometimes, though, a property will need to be sold if it was bought in error. The error could be that over an extended period of time it has not grown in value or that it's costing more to hold each year than you can afford to pay.

The good news is that when the economy struggles and the majority of the world is either in recession or close to it, there is no need to change your buy-and-hold strategy. Try not to read the papers or watch television, with their doom and gloom reports, and try to speak only to fellow investors rather than family or friends who are not in the market. The important thing is not to get caught up in the market bumps, interest rate adjustments and government changes along the way.

History says that well-positioned property, bought for the long-term, is a great investment. Property will always appreciate in value over time.

Overcoming Fears

There are a number of fears you will need to overcome during your journey to wealth, the chief among which is the fear of poverty. It's the most common fear among those of us who are rental property investors.

Common symptoms of the fear of poverty are:

- **Procrastination** – The habit of putting off to tomorrow what you can do today. This is a major cause of failure to achieve your goals. You may think about purchasing property but you find excuses and place obstacles in your own way so that nothing is ever done;

- **Over-caution** – Looking for the negative side of every situation leads to you thinking and talking about failure instead of concentrating on success;

- **Indecision** – Permitting others to do one's thinking and "sitting on the fence" means you become overwhelmed by other people's opinions and take no action.

Consolidation / Review Period

We're nearing the end of this chapter now, which makes it a good time to go over some of the things we've discussed in a way that will hopefully make the most important parts stick firmly in your mind.

First of all, it's always a good idea to have an available line of credit to take care of unexpected rental property expenses. However, you should never over-extend yourself with too high a level of debt. Constantly review the interest rates and fees you're paying and compare them to those offered by other financiers in the market. Consider refinancing to a lender with a lower interest rate, as long as the savings in interest rates are more than the cost of changing lenders. This applies to both your rental properties and private home.

Consider the purchase of a positive cashflow property to help defray the holding costs of your negatively-geared one(s). The trade-off with these properties is that the capital growth is often lower over the long-term.

We recommend that at the end of each year you reflect on what you have achieved during the past 12 months and whether you are closer to your goal of financial freedom. Also, plan your goals for the coming 12 months and five years. Be aware, though, that it's common to underestimate what can be achieved in five years and overestimate what can be achieved in 12 months.

Ensure that your credit cards are paid off in full each month and try to only put expenses on the credit card you can afford to pay in cash. Credit card interest rates are very high and can quickly bite into your cashflow.

Consider consolidating any other private debts or loans you have – such as car, boat, caravan or furniture loans – that have higher interest rates than your private home loan. This will also save cashflow.

Opportunities to purchase properties

The right time to purchase a rental property is always right now. If you take a long-term buy-and-hold approach then there's no such thing as the perfect time. It is time in the market that counts.

There are, however, some conditions for purchasing and holding rental properties that are especially favourable. These include:

- low interest rates
- residential rents increasing
- low rental vacancy rates.

The benefits of holding property over time

Investors who have owned their properties for several years generally find their negatively-geared properties become positively-geared. For instance, we bought a rental property in Ringwood for $210,000 in 2001 that was paying a rental of $220 per week. This represents a gross rental yield of 5.44 per cent ($220 x 52 = $11,440 / $210,000).

In 2015 the property was paying a rental of $500 per week. This represents a gross rental yield of 12.38 per cent ($500 x 52 = $26,000 / $210,000). Our current interest rate payable on the loan for this property is 4.99 per cent per annum.

The property would therefore now be positively-geared.

Chapter 11:
Cash Flow Support Strategies Whilst Owning Properties

Consider the use of debt to help with funding the costs of holding rental properties each year. Each of the following four strategies can help you hold your rental properties when times are tough and cashflow is restricted. Feel free to use them but keep in mind that each strategy involves increasing your level of debt to assist with the holding process. This will eat into future capital growth (equity) of the property (ies).

Example 1: Holding costs of rental property each year

•	**Rent received for year**	$15,000
•	**Less : Cash expenses**	
	Bank fees	$300
	Body corporate fees	$1,200
	Council rates	$1,100
	Insurance	$700
	Interest paid	$16,000
	Property agent's commission	$1,200
	Repairs	$1,000
	Water rates	$400
	Total cash expenses	**($21,900)**
	CASH SHORTFALL	**($6,900)**

- The cash shortfall each year of $6,900 can be funded by a line of credit. The line of credit must not be mixed with private funds to maintain the loan's 100 per cent deductibility.

- The interest on the cumulative balance of this LOC would also be claimable. Here is an example, using 10 per cent interest per annum to keep the calculations as easy as possible:

Year	Shortfall	Claimable interest	LOC balance
1	$6,900	$690 ($6,900 x 10%)	$7,590
2	$6,900	$1,449 (($7,590 + $6,900) x 10%)	$15,939
3	$6,900	$2,284 (($15,939 + $6,900) x 10%)	$25,123

- This interest would be claimable against the property outlined above each financial year.

- According to the conclusion in PBR 69725 you are not required to fund the investment property cash shortfall with personal funds. This means you do not have to use your salary to pay the shortfall of holding costs each year.

- You can choose to use this personal money (that you do not need to utilise to fund holding the property) to pay down your non-deductible private home loan.

Example 2 : Claimable interest when building a rental property

The land costs you $240,000, including purchase expenses, while the building costs you an extra $200,000. The timeframe to complete construction is anticipated to be 12 months and it's expected that roughly $22,000 in interest will be paid during this time.

A line of credit for $462,000 can be established to fund the total cost of land and buildings ($440,000) as well as the $22,000 interest payable during the construction period.

As the intended use of the property is for rental purposes, and has been since the land was first purchased, any interest paid from that date is claimable.

Section 2:

What Needs To Be Considered When Deciding Who Should Purchase The Property?

Chapter 12:
In Your Own Name
(Tax Issues & Other Issues to Consider)

When you and your partner are buying a property there are a number of things you need to take into account before deciding who, legally, will make the purchase.

Some of the things you should consider include:

- when the high income earner will retire or become the low income earner

- when any children will reach the age of 18

- how long it will take the property to become positive

- ages and expected incomes of any potential beneficiaries

- how long you intend to hold the property (it will usually be for the long term due to the high costs involved in buying and selling properties). This will also guide you as to when any capital gain may arise on the sale of the property.

We will discuss the various property ownership options taking into consideration two major factors:

1.   Tax Issues, especially if the property runs at a loss (negatively-geared)

2.   Asset Protection Issues, which comes into effect if the tenant or anybody else sues you.

Quite often you need to forego asset protection to get tax effectiveness and vice versa. Ultimately, it comes down to the compromise you're most comfortable with. There is no right or wrong answer. The individual situation of each person and family needs to be taken into account when making these types of decisions. Each must be considered on a case by case basis.

INDIVIDUAL OWNERSHIP

Every day we see people buying properties in their own names, either because they didn't know they could do it differently or because they are purely focused on the short-term tax benefits.

If you purchase a property in your name you are definitely going to receive a tax benefit in the first few years. However, the rent will eventually start to rise and your interest payments may drop, which may lead to the situation where the rental property becomes positive. If the property was purchased in the high income earner's name, the tax will need to be paid by them each year.

Also, if the property is sold for a profit more tax will need to be paid by the high income earner.

1. Tax Issues

Any losses from a rental property can be offset against any other income earned by the individual. The tax refund will be the loss, in dollars, multiplied by the individual's marginal tax rate percentage.

However, any capital gains from the sale of a rental property after receiving the potential 50 per cent capital gains tax discount will be paid by the individual(s) at their applicable marginal tax rate percentage.

Here is a list of tax rates for the 2014 / 2015 tax year:

$0 - $18,200	Nil
$18,201 - $37,000	19% for each $1 over $18,200
$37,001 - $80,000	$3,572 plus 32.50% for each $1 over $37,000
$80,001 - $180,000	$17,547 plus 37% for each $1 over $80,000
$180,001 and over	$54,547 plus 45% for each $1 over $180,000

Please note that Medicare levy of 2 per cent needs to be added to each of the above tax rates listed

Here, then, is an example showing the refund you can get from negative-gearing:

Rent received for year	$15,000
Less : Cash expenses	
Bank fees	$300
Body corporate fees	$1,200
Council rates	$1,100
Insurance	$700
Interest paid	$16,000
Property agents commission	$1,200
Repairs	$1,000
Water rates	$400
Total cash expenses	($21,900)
CASH SHORTFALL	**($6,900)**
Less : Non-cash expenses	
Decline in value (depreciation)	$3,700
Capital works deduction	$3,300
Borrowing costs amortised	$500
Total non-cash expenses	($7,500)
TOTAL RENTAL PROPERTY LOSS	**($14,400)**
Cash Shortfall Each Year (from above)	**$6,900**

Less: Tax refund

Marginal Tax Rate		Tax Refund	After Tax Cash Shortfall
21.00% ($14,400 x 21.00%)	=	$3,024	$6,900 - $3,024 = $3,876
34.50% ($14,400 x 34.50%)	=	$4,968	$6,900 - $4,968 = $1,932
39.00% ($14,400 x 39.00%)	=	$5,616	$6,900 - $5,616 = $1,284
47.00% ($14,400 x 47.00%)	=	$6,768	$6,900 - $6,768 = $132

Instead of receiving a large tax refund at the end of the financial year, you can apply to vary the tax instalments that your employer deducts before paying your salary each pay period. This is done by lodging a s.1515 variation form with the Australian Tax Office.

The benefit of doing this can be seen in the above example. The cash shortfall was $6,900 each year. The tax refund at 34.50 per cent (which is the bracket that the majority of people fall into) is $4,968. The cash shortfall for the year after the tax refund is $1,932.

By applying to vary your tax instalments from your salary, you are effectively getting that tax refund each pay period instead of in one lump sum after you lodge your tax return. This will help fund the costs of holding the property, which is what makes it an option I prefer.

Some may choose to receive the lump sum refund at the end of the year, as a means of forced savings. That is, if they receive a small amount each pay period the money may be easily wasted whereas a lump sum will be better utilised.

If you are planning to lodge an s.1515 Variation with the tax office, it will only take affect each year from 1 July to 30 June. A new one will need to be prepared for each new financial year.

You need to allow at least 28 days for the form to be processed by the tax office. It can be lodged electronically via the internet.

2. Asset Protection Issues

A high proportion of taxpayers fall into the 34.50 % tax bracket – that is, with taxable incomes ranging between $37,000 and $80,000 – for the 2015 tax year.

From the above example, it would cost them $1,932 per year after tax refund ($37 per week) or $6,900 per year ignoring the tax refund ($133 per week).

The difference between the two is the tax refund of $4,968 or $96 per week. This is effectively the price of asset protection, which means holding the property in a trust instead of holding the property personally.

There is no asset protection at all. The tenant or anybody else who sues you can attack any assets that are in your name or your share of what is held in joint names.

To minimise your exposure you need to ensure you have a mortgage as high as possible on every one of your personal assets and your share of jointly owned assets. This ensures that your personal net worth is as low as possible, preferably set at zero.

Chapter 13:
In a Company Name
(Tax Issues & Other Issues to Consider)

A company is a separate legal entity and exists independently of the directors and shareholders (owners). The most common type is a Pty Ltd company.

The company is divided into ownership portions, each of which is called a share. Having shares gives you ownership rights, meaning that part of the company belongs to you. Directors control and are responsible for the company but are not necessarily the shareholders.

Provided that the annual reporting and tax obligations are met, a company can continue forever. It can own assets and borrow money, as well as sue and be sued.

Assets owned by the company can be attacked by litigants, as can the director(s) of the company. Usually the director(s) can hide behind the "corporate veil" and be protected from being sued by the company. However, the tax office does have the power to go behind the company and personally sue the directors where the company owes the tax office any money. A director can also be personally liable if the company continues to trade whilst insolvent (meaning the company cannot pay debts when they are due).

Administration of companies includes:

- keeping the statutory registers up to date (this is where all directors' and shareholders' minutes are signed and filed)

- checking the annual information / statement provided by ASIC, which oversees the conduct of all companies, and paying the annual filing fee to ASIC

- preparation of annual financials and tax return.

1. Tax Issues

Any losses are trapped inside the company and can be offset against any other income earned by the company in its own right. You should be aware, though, that there are strict rules you need to stick to in order for losses to be carried forward in a company.

Any profits in a company are taxed at the flat rate of 30 % and there is no income splitting that is readily available to companies. Please note that you can personally earn up to $80,000 and pay tax at the maximum marginal rate of 34.50 %, compared to the company's flat rate of 30 % for the 2015 tax year.

Companies do not qualify for the 50% capital gains tax discount and will therefore pay 30% tax on the full profit. Purchasing long-term buy-and-hold assets, such as rental properties, in a company is not a great idea.

The only way to get profits out of a company is via dividends given to shareholders after tax has already been paid. This may lead to tax being personally paid by the shareholder(s) on the dividend being received.

Here's an example:

Profit for year	$10,000
Tax payable at 30 %	$3,000
Profit after tax	$7,000

Note: A fully franked dividend of $7,000 can be paid to shareholders (including an imputation credit of $3,000).

Your taxable income	$60,000
Tax refund	$3,500

You now receive a $7,000 fully franked dividend with an imputation credit of $3,000.

Taxable income now	$70,000 ($60,000 + ($7,000 + $3,000))
Tax payable on dividend	$3,450 ($10,000 x 34.50%)
Less: imputation credit	$3,000
Additional tax on dividend	$450
Tax refund after dividend	$3,050 ($3,500 - $450)

2. Asset Protection Issues

As a shareholder, you are entitled to receive dividends from the company.

The shares held by you in the company are also deemed to be part of your assets if you are sued by a tenant or anyone else who personally sues you. Your shares have a value that depends on what assets are held in the company itself. For example, if the company owns a rental property that has a market value today of $500,000 but also has a mortgage of $300,000 against it, then the property has a net worth of $200,000. If the tenant sues the company the net worth of $200,000 is at risk.

If you're the sole shareholder and someone personally sues you, your shares are worth $200,000 in the example outlined above. These shares become part of your personal assets and are at risk of being lost to the suing party.

Therefore, the asset protection provided by companies depends on whom or what owns the share(s) of the company.

Your accountant can easily help you establish a company, taking the stress and hassles out of the process. You will need to set up the company, sign all the appropriate documents and create a bank account in the name of the company.

Chapter 14:
In a Trust Name
(General Considerations)

A trust lasts for 80 years, during which time the trustee holds the trust property for the beneficiaries.

The trustee, usually a company, is the legal owner of the property and anyone who receives a distribution(s) from the trust is a beneficiary. The beneficiaries cannot be held liable for the actions of the trust.

The trust owns the assets and, because there are no shareholders (unlike a company), there is no actual owner of the trust. The trust is a separate legal entity that can sue and be sued.

Trusts are used mainly to protect assets, though tax minimisation is also possible. This is done because, in the event of legal action, it is the trustee of the trust that is sued.

If the trust is sued, the trustee company has the right to be indemnified out of the assets of the trust. For example:

- the trust is sued for $1,000,000 by the tenant of the property that the trust owns

- the trust owns one rental property which is worth $900,000

- there is a mortgage on the property of $400,000

- thus, the trust has net assets of $500,000 ($900,000 - $400,000)

- the trustee company can access the net assets of the trust – $500,000 – first to settle the tenant's $1,000,000 law suit

- this leaves a shortfall of $500,000.

Because of the shortfall, the lawsuit will go up to the trustee company and attack its assets to satisfy the remaining $500,000 of the lawsuit. However, the trustee company's only asset will be its issued shares (which could be anything from $12 –$120). Thus the remainder of the lawsuit will fail.

At that stage the appointor (discussed below) will sack the current trustee company and appoint a new one. Thus a new trustee takes control of the assets of the trust.

Elements of a trust

- Settlor – Most trusts have a settlor who establishes the trust through a gift of property, often little more than $10. This person cannot benefit from the trust at all and is often the accountant.

- Trustee – Is the legal representative of the trust and has to administer the trust in accordance with the terms of the trust deed. Makes decisions about the trust, such as what to invest in and who to distribute to. Trustees can be individuals or a company, though we would strongly advise against an individual taking on the role. If a tenant sues and the assets of the trust aren't enough to cover the lawsuit, the individual trustee's personally assets are potentially at risk. This is why a corporate trustee should always be used.

- Powers of trustee – These are dependant on the trust deed. The trust can often buy assets, borrow, set up bank accounts and carry out other similar tasks.

- Liability of trustee – The trustee is personally liable for the debts which they incur on behalf of the trust. The trustee does have the right to be indemnified out of the trust's assets, as discussed above.

- Trust deed – This governs the trustee, listing the powers and rights of the trustee, beneficiaries and others. The deed may be varied by a deed of variation.

- Appointor – Holds the power of the trust, with the ability to hire or fire the trustee. You have to carefully consider who has this role.

- Beneficiaries – These are usually named in the trust deed. The trustee has the discretion to choose who to distribute the profits of the trust to (provided it is a discretionary trust).

Administration of trusts with a trustee company includes:

- keeping the statutory registers up to date of the company (this is where all directors and shareholders minutes are signed and filed, etc.)

- checking the annual information / statement provided by ASIC for the company and paying the annual filing fee to ASIC, which oversees the conduct of all companies

- preparation of annual financials and tax return for the trust and beneficiaries.

Your accountant can easily help you establish a trustee company and trust.

Set-up issues:

Please note that you will need to set up both the trustee company and trust, sign all the appropriate documents, create a bank account in the name of the trust and get the trust deed stamped (if required) at the State Revenue Office in the state in which your trust was established. This will all need to occur before you can sign a contract to purchase a property in the name of the trust.

The bank account will need to be established as follows: "ABC Pty Ltd as Trustee for ABC Trust."

The name on the property purchase contract will also be: "ABC Pty Ltd as Trustee for ABC Trust".

Once again, the loan from the bank for the property purchase would also be to: "ABC Pty Ltd as Trustee for ABC Trust"

(note: "As Trustee for" can also be shortened to "ATF".)

One thing you mustn't overlook is the updating of your wills once the trust and trustee company have been established. A company has directors and shareholders, while a trust has an appointor, all of whom are usually yourself and/or your family members. Your will needs to cater for the transfer of such positions upon the death of yourself or your spouse.

Chapter 15:
In a Trust Name: Unit Trust
(Tax Issues & Other Issues to Consider)

This is a trust in which all beneficiaries have, by virtue of their holdings of units in the trust, a fixed entitlement to the income and capital of the trust. It's similar to companies issuing shares to shareholders, except units are issued to unitholders.

1. Tax Issues

Any losses are trapped inside the unit trust. They can be offset against any other income earned by the unit trust in its own right.

Any profits in a unit trust are distributed to the unitholder in direct proportion to their unitholding percentage, as no income splitting is readily available. You can personally earn up to $80,000 and pay tax at the maximum marginal rate of 34.50 %. For example, if there are 120 units issued and you own 60 of them, you will receive 50 % of the profits from the unit trust. You will therefore pay tax on the distribution at the appropriate marginal tax rate percentage, as discussed earlier.

Unit trusts do qualify for the 50 per cent capital gains tax discount.

Sometimes with trusts like these the borrowing is kept outside the trust.

To give you an example:

Profit for year	$10,000
Your taxable income	$60,000
Tax refund	$3,500

You now receive a $10,000 distribution from the unit trust, as sole unitholder.

Taxable income now	$70,000 ($60,000 + $10,000)
Tax payable on distribution	$3,450 ($10,000 x 34.50%)
Additional tax on distribution	$3,450
Tax refund after distribution	$50 ($3,500 original refund - $3,450)

If, on the other hand, you have borrowed to buy your units it would look like this:

You, the sole unitholder have borrowed to buy your units. The loan will therefore be in your name.

Interest paid during the year for this loan	$15,000.
Taxable income (original)	$60,000 (as above)
Plus: Distribution received	$10,000
Less: Loan Interest paid	$15,000
Adjusted Taxable Income	$55,000 ($60,000 + $10,000 – $15,000)
Your taxable income now decreases by	$5,000 ($60,000 - $55,000)
Additional tax refund	$1,725 ($5,000 decrease x 34.50%)
Tax refund after distribution and interest	$5,225 ($3,500 + $1,725)

2. Asset Protection Issues

As a unitholder, you are entitled to receive distributions from the unit trust.

The units held by you in the unit trust are also deemed to be part of your assets if you are sued by a tenant or anyone else who personally sues you.

Your units also have a value on them depending on what assets are held in the unit trust itself. For instance, if the unit trust owns a rental property that has a market value today of $500,000 and also has a mortgage of $300,000 against it then the property has a net worth of $200,000. If the tenant sues the unit trust this money is also at risk.

Also, if someone personally sues you then your units, worth $200,000, become part of your personal assets for the suing party and are at risk.

Therefore, the asset protection provided by unit trusts depends upon who or what owns the unit(s).

Chapter 16:
In a Trust Name: Discretionary Trust / Family Trust (Tax Issues & Other Issues to Consider)

This is a trust in which no beneficiaries have any fixed rights to income and capital of the trust. The trust is held for the beneficiaries and distributed at the trustee's discretion.

Anyone who has a business or some other income source has a big advantage, as they can obtain tax effectiveness and asset protection too.

The trust provides the maximum flexibility when distributing income and capital gains made in any given tax year.

Therefore, it can be summarised as follows:

- you could be the director and shareholder of the company. This means you control the company but that you personally own nothing;

- the company is the trustee for the trust that owns everything. Therefore, as director of the trustee you control the trust;

- the trust distributes all profits to beneficiaries, who you nominate. That could be yourself, spouse, children, parents or anybody at all;

- to put it as simply as possible, you own nothing but control everything.

1. Tax Issues

To begin with, discretionary trusts qualify for the 50 % capital gains tax discount.

Any losses are trapped inside the discretionary trust and can be offset against any other income earned by the discretionary trust in its own right.

If another discretionary trust makes a profit for the year then – as long as both trust deeds allow – the trust with the profit can distribute to the trust with the loss to offset the loss and save tax on the profit.

For any profits left in the discretionary trust, which are not distributed to beneficiaries, the trust will pay tax at the top marginal rate – currently 47.00 %.

Any profits in a discretionary trust therefore need to be distributed each year to the beneficiaries. You should be aware that income splitting is readily available in discretionary trusts. You can personally earn up to $80,000 in a tax year and pay tax at the maximum marginal rate of 34.50 per cent, so you will pay tax on the distribution at your appropriate marginal tax rate percentage as discussed earlier.

Each year the trustee can choose who to distribute the profits of the trust to. Those who can be beneficiaries, depending on how the trust deed has been written, include:

- you
- your spouse
- your children
- yours or your spouse's parents
- yours or your spouse's grandparents
- your grandchildren
- brothers and sisters of you and your spouse
- nieces and nephews of you and your spouse
- other discretionary trusts that any of the above are beneficiaries of
- other companies that the above are directors or shareholders of.

Potentially distributing to a company (also known as a bucket company) will help cap the tax rate on the distributions from the trust at the company's tax rate, being 30%.

You can also potentially distribute some of the trust's income to minors, if so allowed by the trust deed and its definition of beneficiaries. A minor is a child under the age of 18 at June 30 each tax year.

A minor can only earn $416 each year without the need to pay any tax at all:

Don't forget, though, to allow for any income they may earn already from bank interest or any dividends they may receive. You must take this into account to keep the minor under the relevant income threshold.

The trustee can also choose to distribute to those adult beneficiaries who are over 18 and who pay tax at a lower marginal rate than you or your spouse. Over many years these tax savings can add up to tens of thousands of dollars.

2. Asset Protection Issues

This trust offers the best form of asset protection available because none of the beneficiaries has a fixed right to any income or capital distribution paid by the trust. This means that creditors cannot force the trustee to distribute to them at all.

To go back to our early example, assume the discretionary trust owns a rental property that has a market value today of $500,000 and also has a mortgage of $300,000 against it. This leaves the property with a net worth of $200,000 that is at risk if the tenant sues.

If someone personally sues you then the assets of the discretionary trust are not at risk, for the reasons outlined above. Therefore, the assets of the discretionary trust worth $200,000 cannot become part of your personal assets for the suing party and are not at risk at all.

However, if you have several rental properties in the one trust and a tenant sues that trust, the total equity owned by all the properties is at risk in the law suit. One way around this is to buy each rental property in a separate trust, thus minimising the risk in each trust to only the property owned within it. This is the approach that we personally utilise.

HYBRID TRUST

Hybrid trusts have been popular due to the fact they offer potential tax benefits and asset protection. A hybrid trust deed has the elements of both a unit trust and a discretionary trust.

The taxpayer claims the interest deduction as a unit holder of a unit trust whilst it is negatively-geared. However, when the investment becomes positively-geared the trust then acts as a discretionary trust, allowing you to distribute the income to family members who are at a lower marginal rate.

In response to the increased use of hybrid trust arrangements, the ATO has significantly increased its interest in this area. The tax office will probably negate any benefits of this type of trust, which will not make them viable at all. Therefore, we're not going to cover this type of trust.

Section 3:

**Maximising Your Money For Retirement
By Utilising A Self-Managed Super Fund (SMSF)**

Chapter 17:
Benefits of a SMSF & the $200,000 Myth

We're all ageing...whether we like it or not. As we get older and start thinking about retirement, good health becomes the most important thing that we have, and rightly so. The bodies we've been given need to last us a lifetime.

For most, thoughts of retirement also conjure up images of relaxing on beaches, travel and finally being able to realise lifelong dreams. But how many of us will actually have enough money to live the lifestyle we desire in our latter years? Not many.

With Australia's ageing population, it's more important than ever before to secure your retirement lifestyle choices now by building wealth. A self-managed super fund is a powerful vehicle by which this can potentially be achieved.

The benefits of having your own Self-Managed Super Fund are:

- CONTROL over where your money is being invested

- A FAMILY FUND where up to four members of your family can reap the rewards

- A SECURE INCOME IN RETIREMENT

- INVESTMENT CHOICE

- You can PURCHASE INVESTMENT PROPERTY using a Self-Managed Super Fund

- TAXATION BENEFITS

- FLEXIBILITY to make changes to your investment strategy as you need to

- Greater SECURITY for you and your family with sustainable life and permanent disability insurance

- The right PROTECTION in place to secure your Super

- You can PURCHASE BUSINESS PREMISES

Why it works so well:

- SMSF's pay the least tax; being taxed at only 15%

- If you hold an asset for over 12 months and then sell it, you pay only 10% tax on the profit

- SMSF's that are 100% in pension mode, are tax free

- Life insurance & Total and Permanent Disability (TPD) insurance & Income Protection insurance can all be paid and deducted by the SMSF

- Assets are protected within your SMSF – creditors can't touch your superannuation

The $200,000 Myth:

It is often thought that a minimum of $200,000 is needed to establish a new SMSF.

In many instances a superannuation balance of well below the $200,000 threshold is more than adequate for transitioning into an SMSF.

This in turn is opening up the viability of SMSFs to a higher proportion of Australian workers.

Please see our example below of purchasing a property in an SMSF.

Chapter 18:
Questions to Ask Yourself

Questions to ask yourself if you are considering setting up a Self-Managed Super Fund:

- What is your current age?

- How much money do you have to roll into your SMSF?

- How much do you have to contribute to your SMSF on a regular basis including contributions and rollovers to cover the annual running costs of the Fund?

- Do you own share investments in your own name? If yes, would you consider transferring these share investments into your SMSF?

- Is one of the reasons you are thinking of obtaining your own SMSF to have control over where your money is invested?

- Do you wish to know more about the benefits of purchasing an investment property within your SMSF?

- Do you want to have control over the amount of life insurance held on your behalf? If so, how much cover would you obtain?

Questions to ask yourself if you have an existing Self-Managed Super Fund:

- Do you have more than $130,000 currently in your SMSF?

- Are you happy with the current rate of return on your SMSF?

- Do you wish to know more about the benefits of purchasing an investment property within your SMSF?

- Have you considered other family members reaping the rewards with you?

- Are you maximising your fund's growth potential by ensuring all members have their 9.5% (from 1st July 2014) mandatory employer contributions paid into the SMSF?

- Did you know that having your life insurance paid by your SMSF allows you to obtain more substantial cover to meet your personal needs?

- Does your Total and Permanent Disability insurance within your SMSF meet the 'any occupation' definition?

- Did you know you can claim your Income Protection Insurance as an SMSF deduction?

- Are all of the investment expenses being claimed as a deduction within the SMSF?

- Is the SMSF Deed current?

- Does your SMSF have a current investment strategy in place?

Chapter 19:
Example of How a Property in a SMSF can Increase Your Retirement Nest Egg by $824,000:

All you need is as little as $130,000 in Super and you can buy an investment property worth $450,000.

The SMSF borrows up to 80% of the purchase price	$360,000
SMSF contribution towards the purchase	$90,000
Stamp Duty, Legal Costs & set up costs	$40,000

**Let's say the price of the property doubles every 10 years
20 years later, your property is now worth**

$1,800,000!

Now sell it...

Gross Capital Gain is a staggering (before any CGT discount)	**$1,350,000**
Assuming tax is paid at 10% ... TAX PAID (after allowing for CGT discount)	**$135,000**

Extra money for retirement in 20 years...

$1,305,000!!

(BEING $1,800,000 LESS $360,000 DEBT LESS $135,000 TAX)

So, what does the $130,000 get you if left invested with shares and managed funds?

Let's say prices double every 10 years
20 years later ... it's now worth

$520,000

(INCLUDING DIVIDENDS AND TAX BENEFITS OF RE-INVESTING)

Now sell it...

Gross Capital Gain is (before any CGT discount)	$390,000
Assuming tax is paid at 10% ... TAX PAID (after allowing for CGT discount)	$39,000

Extra money for retirement in 20 years...

$481,000!!

(BEING $520,000 LESS $39,000 TAX)

THEREFORE A <u>PROPERTY PURCHASE</u> COULD EARN YOU $824,000 MORE FOR RETIREMENT THAN SHARES COULD!

Chapter 20:
SMSF's explained

Advantages and Disadvantages of Property Investment

Advantages

- Property can be less volatile than shares or other investments

- You can earn rental income and benefit from capital growth (if your property increases in value over time)

- If you take out a loan to purchase an investment property, interest on the loan and most property expenses can be offset against rental income, for tax purposes

- You are investing in something you can see and touch

Disadvantages

- Rental income may not cover your mortgage payments or other expenses so you may have to use other money to cover these costs

- An increase in interest rates will increase your repayments and decrease your disposable income

- There may be periods of time where you don't have a tenant and will have to cover all costs yourself

- You can't sell off a bedroom if you need to access some cash in a hurry

- There are very high entry and exit costs such as stamp duty, legal fees and real estate agent's fees

SMSF Property Rules: The Property

- Must meet the Sole Purpose Test (as discussed below)

- Must not be acquired from a related party or member#

- Must not be lived in by a fund member or any fund members' related parties

- Must not be rented by a fund member or any fund members' related parties

---

HINT#

The SMSF could potentially purchase your business premises, allowing you to pay rent directly to your SMSF at the market rate

---

HINT

You have to be very careful when buying property via an SMSF as only certain types of repairs and / or renovations are allowed under the law

---

Summary of General Issues For Using A Self-Managed Super Fund (Smsf)

General

A Self-Managed Superannuation Fund (SMSF) gives you the opportunity to actively manage your own superannuation.

The trustees hold and invest the assets of the SMSF for the benefit of the members.

An SMSF has:

- Four or fewer members

- The members themselves act as trustees (except for single member funds) and

- No trustee receives any remuneration for their services as trustees

If your fund has individual trustees, the following must apply:

- it has four or less members

- each member is a trustee (if there is one member, two trustees are needed)

- no trustee is paid for their duties or services as a trustee

If your fund has a corporate trustee, the following apply:

- it has four or less members

- each member of the fund is a Director of the company

- each Director of the corporate trustee is a member of the fund

- the corporate trustee is not paid for its services as a trustee

- no Director of the corporate trustee is paid for their duties or services as Director in relation to the fund.

Sole Purpose Test

This means your fund needs to be maintained for the sole purpose of providing retirement benefits to your members, or to their dependents if a member dies before retirement. As a trustee, you need to maintain your SMSF so that it complies with the sole purpose test at all times while your SMSF exists, including when investing fund assets and paying benefits upon retirement of members.

Single member funds

If you have a corporate trustee for a single member fund, the member needs to be one of the following:

- the sole Director of the trustee company

You can also have two individuals as trustees. One trustee needs to be the member and the other needs to be one of the following:

- a person related to the member

A trustee or Director can't be paid for their services as a trustee or Director in relation to the fund.

Obligations

You are ultimately responsible for running your SMSF. As a trustee of an SMSF, you need to act according to the following:

- your fund's trust deed
- the provisions of the super laws,
- other general rules, such as those imposed under other tax and trust laws.

If you are a new trustee or newly appointed Director of a corporate trustee, you need to sign the Trustee Declaration within 21 days of your appointment to show that you understand your duties as a trustee of an SMSF.

Money belonging to your SMSF can't be used for personal or business purposes under any circumstances. The SMSF's assets are not a form of credit or emergency fund when faced with a sudden need and should never be used as such as the penalties applicable can be severe.

IF YOU DON'T FOLLOW THE RULES, YOU RISK ONE OR MORE OF THE FOLLOWING:

- your SMSF being deemed non-compliant and losing its tax concessions
- getting disqualified as a trustee

- prosecution
- penalties

IF YOU FAIL TO ACT ACCORDING TO THE TRUST DEED, OTHER MEMBERS OF YOUR FUND MAY TAKE LEGAL ACTION AGAINST YOU.

Types of contributions

1. Employer Compulsory Contributions
2. Your Voluntary Contributions (such as salary sacrifice)
3. Contributions as a self-employed person
4. Contributions from the Government (Co-Contributions)

Rollovers

An SMSF can accept a rollover from a superannuation fund that you are a member of currently. This way you can rollover your balances in other super accounts into your SMSF account.

Managing your fund's investments

You need to prepare and implement and sign an investment strategy for your fund, and review it regularly.

The strategy needs to reflect the purpose and circumstances of your fund and consider the following:

- investing in a way to maximise member returns taking into account the risk associated with the investment
- diversification and the benefits of investing across a number of asset classes (for example, shares, property and fixed deposit) in a long-term investment strategy
- the ability of your fund to pay benefits as members retire and pay other costs incurred by your fund
- the needs of members (for example, age, income level, employment pattern and retirement needs)

The investment strategy should set out your investment objectives and detail the investment methods you'll adopt to achieve these objectives. You need to make sure all investment decisions are made according to the investment strategy of your fund. If in any doubt, you should seek investment advice or appoint an investment manager in writing.

Restrictions

Super laws place restrictions on the types of entities your fund can invest in or with, and the entities that your fund can acquire assets from. Investment restrictions exist because they protect fund members by making sure fund assets are not exposed to undue risks, like a business failing.

Assets / Loans / Borrowing

- You need to ensure that your fund's ownership of its investments is secure

- A member cannot use or benefit from any asset owned by an SMSF

- You cannot acquire assets for your fund from a related party of your fund, however, limited exceptions do apply like listed shares and managed funds

- You cannot lend money or provide direct or indirect financial help (including the provision of credit) from your fund, to a member, or a member's relative

- You can only borrow money in very limited circumstances like Instalment Warrants

Paying Benefits to Members

Cashing of benefits

Compulsory

- Only when a member dies

Voluntary

- **Preserved benefits** may be cashed voluntarily only if a condition of release is met and then subject to any cashing restrictions imposed by the super laws. Cashing restrictions tell you what form the benefits need to be taken in

- **Restricted non-preserved benefits** can't be cashed until the member meets a condition of release. They are subject to the same cashing restrictions as preserved benefits, exceptions may apply

- **Unrestricted non-preserved benefits** don't require a condition of release to be met, and may be paid upon demand by the member. For example, where a member has previously satisfied a condition of release and decided to keep the money in the Super fund

Member benefits may generally be paid in any of the following forms:

- a single lump sum

- one or more pensions or the purchase of one or more annuities

Conditions of release

Preserved benefits and restricted non-preserved benefits may be paid out for the following reasons:

1. Retirement
2. Attaining age 65 or more (Note - payments can be made to those over 55 with certain conditions)
3. Permanent incapacity
4. Temporary incapacity
5. Severe financial hardship
6. Compassionate grounds

7. Temporary residents departing Australia

8. Transition to retirement (attaining preservation age)

9. Terminal illness or injury

10. Rollovers and transfers

Reporting and Administration Obligations

Annual Tax Return

All SMSFs need to lodge an SMSF annual return with the ATO each year, in order to:

- report income tax
- report super regulatory information
- report member contributions
- pay the supervisory levy

Member contributions

You need to report all contributions you receive for each member in the SMSF annual tax return.

Rollover benefits statement

A Rollover benefits statement needs to be completed.

Supervisory levy

SMSFs need to pay the ATO their supervisory levy every year, which is included in the SMSF annual tax return

Appoint an approved auditor

As a trustee of an SMSF, you are required to appoint an approved auditor to audit your fund each year, at least 30 days before the due date of the SMSF annual return. Your auditor is required to:

- examine your fund's financial statements

- assess your fund's overall compliance with the Super law

Australian Financial Services Licence (AFSL)

Anyone who gives advice on an SMSF must hold an AFSL licence. You can research on ASIC's professional register to see if the company or person holds the AFSL

Record Keeping Requirements

You need to keep the following records for a minimum of 10 years:

- minutes of trustee meetings and decisions (where matters affecting your fund were discussed)

- records of all changes of trustees - trustee declarations recognising the obligations and responsibilities for any trustee, or Director of a corporation

- trustee, appointed after 30 June 2007

- members' written consent to be appointed as trustees

- copies of all reports given to members

Once you've established your fund, you are legally required to:

- lodge an SMSF annual tax return

- pay the supervisory levy year

- have an audit report prepared year

- notify the ATO within 28 days of any changes to trustees, Directors, members, contact details or fund status

You have to do this each financial year, including the year you establish your SMSF.

Compliance

To ensure that an SMSF remains compliant and that penalties are not enforced, it is imperative that all obligations are met, those being:

- Keep and maintain accurate records of your SMSF

- Don't set up an SMSF with the expectation of gaining early access to Super

- Don't make false or misleading statements or fail to make a statement to avoid paying the correct income tax

- Lodge your SMSF annual return every financial year and pay the supervisory levy

Corporate or Individual Trustee?

Corporate

Advantages	Disadvantages
Member additions or deletions, is a simple form with ASIC	Member under 18 years old, cannot be a Director or a corporate trustee.
Corporate trustee survives the death of a member	If a corporate trustee also trades or is a trustee for another entity, they can be at risk of creditors, unless the trust deed makes a provision for members to appoint others as the trustee.
If single member fund, the member can be the sole Director of the corporate trustee	Additional cost – ASIC annual review fee $46 (as at 31st December 2015)
Estate Planning	
Obtaining Finance on investments	
Benefit payments are not limited due to trustee.	

Individual

Advantages	Disadvantages
Reduced costs	Member additions or deletions, means all the assets held in the SMSF will need to be updated, to include a new member, or to remove a member. i.e. Contact bank to change the bank account to have all current members as trustees
Member under 18 years old can be a trustee	If a member dies, there are limited means to continue the fund, especially if a single member fund
	If a single member fund, another trustee needs to be listed
	Difficulty in efficient estate planning
	Difficult/impossible to obtain finance on investments
	Sole purpose of the fund will be to provide age pensions and not lump sum benefits

Before making the decision we recommend discussing with both your accountant and your solicitor.

Chapter 21:
Bare Trusts Explained

Installment Warrant (Bare Trust) Flowchart Summary

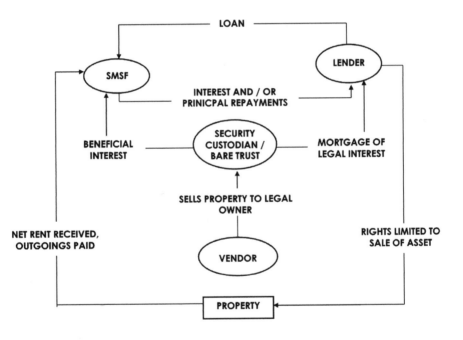

Availability:

- New loans only
- Investment purposes only
- Loans secured by a first registered mortgage only

Not Available for:

- Owner-occupied property
- Renovations or repairs or improvements
- Increases
- Building loans
- Refinances (still awaiting clarification on this)

KEY ISSUES / REQUIREMENTS:

Loan is by the Super fund

The SMSF borrows the money and makes any principal and / or interest repayments. (This is even though the actual money is lent by the financier to the Bare Trust).

Loan is applied for the purchase of an asset

A loan can only be applied for the purchase of an asset only. Be careful not to borrow for improvement or development of assets.

Asset must be one in which the SMSF is permitted to buy

Permits borrowing to finance investment in assets that are allowed to be bought outright under Super laws.

Asset is held on trust and the SMSF acquires a beneficial interest in the asset

Legal Title on purchase is held by the Bare Trust. This will be the case until the loan is fully repaid. The beneficial interest remains with the

96

SMSF. That is, the SMSF receives the rent, pays all costs of owning the asset including interest and pays tax on any Capital Gains from the sale of the asset in the future.

The SMSF can acquire the legal ownership of the asset after the loan is fully repaid

The SMSF can choose to, but does not have to, acquire legal ownership once it has fully repaid the loan.

Non-Recourse Loan from financier

This means that in the event of default, the lender may sell or take title to the asset to meet the Super fund trustees' liabilities. The lender cannot take action against the fund's trustees to recover the loss suffered by the lender in any circumstances.

Finance

Lenders will typically charge a higher interest rate than normal and will accept lower loan-to-value ratios (LVR) because of the non-recourse nature of these loans.

Security Custodian (Bare Trust)

The asset being bought is held on trust for the SMSF while the loan is being repaid. This relationship is also known as a "Bare Trust".

The Bare Trust should have a Company as trustee. All members of the SMSF should be Directors and shareholders of the Bare Trust's trustee company. This company should not be a trading company either.

The SMSF cannot have the same trustees as the Bare Trust's trustee company. Therefore, if the SMSF has a company trustee already, then a new company is required for the Bare Trust.

The Bare Trust should play as minimal a role as possible in the borrowing arrangement (that is, only hold the legal title and nothing else)

There is no need for the Bare Trust to open a bank account, apply for a tax file number, lodge a tax return, or do anything other than hold the title to the asset for the SMSF until the loan is fully repaid. The company that is trustee for the Bare Trust does not need a public officer either. THE BARE TRUST BEING ACTIVE IN ANY WAY SHOULD BE AVOIDED AT ALL COSTS.

Who Signs Contract to Purchase?

The Trustee of the Bare Trust is the entity that holds the title to the property on trust for the Super Fund. Therefore, it is the Bare Trust's Trustee that should be noted as the purchaser of the property on the contract of sale, NOT the Super Fund or the Super Fund Trustee.

Each state has different requirements regarding the manner in which the Bare Trust's Trustee is noted on the contract. In some states, the name of the Bare Trust's Trustee alone is sufficient, whereas other states require a greater amount of detail (for example, the name of the Bare Trust and the Super Fund).

Whilst the above may seem long winded, it shows that the Bare Trust is holding the property on trust for the Super Fund.

PLEASE SPEAK WITH YOUR SOLICITOR AND THE RESPECTIVE STATE REVENUE OFFICE IN YOUR STATE BEFORE COMPLETING AND SIGNING A PURCHASE CONTRACT. THIS ENSURES THAT ALL STAMP DUTY OBLIGATIONS ARE MINIMISED FOR THE SMSF.

Double Stamp Duty

As long as the name of the purchaser on the contract has been correctly noted (as per above) and the Instalment Warrant Deed has been used and signed correctly, there should not be any more stamp duty charged at the point in time when the legal title passes from the Bare Trust to the SMSF (that is, when the loan is fully repaid).

Goods and Services Tax (GST)

The activities of the Bare Trust are considered essentially passive in nature and that true "Bare Trusts" do not carry on businesses and therefore are not required to register for GST.

Capital Gains Tax

When the loan is fully repaid, the transfer of legal title to the asset from the Bare Trust to the SMSF should not constitute a change in ownership (provided that the documentation is correctly completed as per above because the SMSF has always held beneficial ownership in the asset.)

Therefore no CGT should arise on this transfer. This highlights the need for the Bare Trust to engage in only minimal activities to ensure a CGT event does not arise on transfer of legal title to the SMSF.

If the property is sold at any stage to a third party, any Capital Gains tax will be payable by the SMSF.

Interest Claims

Interest will be deductible to the SMSF as long as it is paid to receive rent on the property and will continue to be deductible as long as the property is available for rent or is actually being rented out.

Lease Agreement

Although the Bare Trust should be named on the lease, the tenant (or agent if managed by one) should pay the rent direct to the SMSF as beneficial owner.

Insurance

Requirements of insurers may vary. If the insurer requires the policy to be in the name of the Bare Trust's Trustee, then do so but the policy should record that the SMSF has a beneficial interest in the property. All premiums should be paid by the SMSF.

Other General SMSF Issues and Tax Issues

After the SMSF settles on the property, the SMSF receives the rent and pays all running costs such as interest, council rates, repairs, agent's commission, body corporate fees, insurance, etc.

An SMSF is able to claim any depreciation deduction entitlements too. Please consider if there are any entitlements and consult a quantity surveyor to prepare a report for your SMSF.

Property Purchase Locations

The geographic locations in which you can purchase property may be restricted by the lender. Please check with the lender before deciding on a particular area that you are considering buying a property in. Consider getting the potential location approved by the lender as part of the pre-approval process.

Guarantees

The Tax Office has voiced their concerns about additional guarantees (that is, personal guarantees). These guarantees are considered contrary to the intent of these types of borrowing arrangements. Clarification on guarantees is still yet to be provided by the Tax Office. It is considered best to avoid any personal guarantees.

Chapter 22:
Process for Purchase of a Property
with Super (including documentation)

Process for SMSF Wanting To Purchase Property via an Instalment Warrant:

1. An SMSF is set up with the appropriate powers to borrow and invest in residential and / or commercial property. Ensure the SMSF deed is allowed to borrow through a limited recourse loan.

2. If necessary, the SMSF Trust Deed of an existing fund is amended to allow the SMSF to borrow and to invest in residential and / or commercial property per point above.

3. The SMSF checks that the investment being considered is an appropriate and permitted investment for their superannuation fund under super laws and their trust deed.

4. Obtain pre-approval for the loan from the financier.

5. The Bare Trust and Company Trustee is established. Please have the Instalment Warrant Deed signed and stamped at the State Revenue Office in your state (if applicable).

6. A property is found and the Bare Trust enters into a Contract of Purchase (possibly subject to finance) – BEING CAREFUL ON WHOSE NAME GOES ON THE CONTRACT (SEE STAMP DUTY SECTION).

7. SMSF applies for a loan and provides supporting documents.

8. Certified copies of the SMSF Trust Deed and Instalment Warrant Deed are forwarded by SMSF to the Bank's panel solicitor to review and certify compliance.

9. Loan Offer Document and security documents are produced and sent for execution.

10. Customer executes and returns:

   a) Loan Offer Document.

   b) Security documents signed by the SMSF Trustees as borrower and the Bare Trust as mortgagor.

11. At settlement funds to complete come from:

   a) Any deposit previously paid (from the SMSF's own funds),

   b) The SMSF's own funds, and

   c) The loan being advanced.

12. The transfer (to the Bare Trust) and the mortgage are registered.

13. After settlement the SMSF rents the property to an unrelated party on commercial terms.

14. The SMSF collects the rent, pays the usual outgoings on the property and makes the loan repayments.

15. When the loan is repaid:

   a) The mortgage is discharged,

   b) The SMSF can receive a transfer of property from the Bare Trust (if it chooses to transfer the title, it does not have to), and

   c) The SMSF can become the registered proprietor if it is transferred by the Bare Trust as per above.

Loan Documentation:

1. The Loan Offer Document should state :

a) That the loan is a limited recourse loan i.e. There will be no recourse to the other assets of the SMSF or to either the SMSF Trustees or to the Bare Trust

b) The borrower must provide the Bank with proof that they have received independent legal advice.

c) The borrower must provide the Bank with proof that they have received independent financial advice

d) Property is to be fully insured against fire and other major hazards

2. The customer must provide a certified copy of the Trust Deed for the SMSF, which will be reviewed by a Bank Panel solicitor

3. The customer must provide a certified copy of the Instalment Warrant Deed, which will be reviewed by a Bank Panel solicitor

4. An undertaking that includes a declaration of compliance with the SIS Act from the SMSF Trustee

Profile - Adrian Hill

"We make the tax man work as hard for you
as you do."

ADRIAN HILL

Adrian Hill is one of only a few accountants talking the talk and walking the walk on the wealth-creation trail. A CPA accountant with 25 years' experience, he is constantly surprised by the amount of hard-earned money that people don't claim back from the tax office.

Adrian's wealth-creation journey began in 2000 when he started reading books and attending seminars on subjects including rental properties as well as share and option trading. He has obtained one of the best financial educations available through traditional means and has spent well over $200,000 on his own independent financial education.

It is through this that he learned how to pay his own home off in full and he has purchased over 20 investment properties and numerous shares. He bought his first rental property in 2001 and has continued to buy property since then. He has traded shares and options over the years and in 2008 undertook a couple of subdivisions.

He and his wife have had their own self-managed super fund (SMSF) since 2004 and they have recently bought their business premises in the SMSF with the help from the bank (via a loan).

Adrian's mission is to minimise tax; he also strongly believes "the tax man should work as hard as you do". It has been his experience that if you don't have a rental property then you don't know the magic that can be achieved. Through learning tricks of the trade, you can legally use the tax laws to your advantage.

He is extremely passionate about properties, taxation reduction strategies and protecting your hard-earned assets. He loves to educate and will gladly spend hours assisting anyone who is willing to take steps towards financial freedom.

In 2004 he founded Superior Accounting Solutions Pty Ltd to do just that, and so far has attracted 100 per cent of clients through referrals. Superior Super Solutions Pty Ltd and Superior Accounting Group were founded in 2013 to provide a more streamlined and tailored solution for super funds. Adrian's team is currently assisting more than 350 like-minded client groups to make the tax man work up a sweat!

Congratulations
& Special Gift Below:

Congratulations on reading this book, you have already come a long way. If you have read this far then you have distinguished yourself from the rest and elevated yourself to the top 1% of investors.

I would like to thank you by providing you with some free resources so that you can continue the momentum that you have created with this book.

Free Gift # 1 – Yearly Budget Template to facilitate a review of all personal income and expenses.

Free Gift # 2 – Rental Property Purchasing Checklist.

Free Gift # 3 – Have a 20 Minute Consultation with one of our high calibre investment property and superannuation specialists (please refer to the website below to choose the appropriate review / session).

To receive the above FREE GIFTS, please register at

www.superioraccountinggroup.com/gifts

Superior Accounting Group

Street Address : 13 Mereweather Avenue, Frankston, Vic, 3930.
Postal Address : PO Box 922, Mount Eliza, Vic, 3930.
Phone : (03) 9787-8906
Fax : (03) 9783-1557
E-mail : customercare@superioraccountinggroup.com
Website : www.superioraccountinggroup.com